Christianity AND WAR

Christianity AND WAR

A SERMON

Setting forth the Sufferings of Christians.
The Origin and Import of the Christian Name,
Christianity and War Considered,
Illustrated and Set Forth.

Also

A Short Address to the Mennonite Brethren,
to Which Are Appended
Several Beautiful and Well Adapted Hymns

By

A MINISTER OF THE OLD MENNONITE CHURCH

John M. Brenneman

We do not war after the flesh,
for the weapons of our warfare are not carnal.
2 Cor. 10:3, 4.

SERMON ON THE MOUNT
PUBLISHING

The main text of this book is in the public domain. Present publisher's additions and cover are copyright © 2017 Sermon on the Mount Publishing.

ISBN 978-1-68001-017-6

For additional titles and other material by the same author, contact:

Sermon on the Mount Publishing
P.O. Box 246
Manchester, MI 48158
(734) 428 – 0488

the-witness@sbcglobal.net
www.kingdomreading.com

Our Mission
To obey the commands of Christ and to teach men to do so.

First Printing— November 2017—800 copies
Second Printing—July 2022—1,250 copies
Third Printing—POD edition

Acknowledgments

The publishers thank the many who have aided in this project in many ways, including: Vincent, Barbara, Faith, and Grace Ste. Marie, for their help in ensuring the accuracy of the text; Joe Springer and the staff of the Mennonite Historical Library, for their able and cheerful aid in finding information and documents; Steven M. Nolt, for providing a copy of Funk's booklet; Chester Weaver, Leonard Gross, and Theron Schlabach, for their helpful comments on the Historical Introduction; Jennifer Burdge, for copy editing; Edsel Burdge, for identifying Brenneman's reference to a Quaker's statement; and Mike Atnip, for design and layout.

May the Lord reward you richly!

Contents

Historical Introduction   *ii*

Christianity and War Considered   *1*

An Address to the Mennonite Brethren.   *34*

A Word to the Careless   *40*

Appendix: Warfare: Its Evils—Our Duty   *44*

Historical Introduction

The Civil War raged on, now in its second year. The toll in human lives and property lost climbed higher and higher. In the North, patriotism and enthusiasm for the war threatened even Mennonites and Amish, and some of their sons enlisted and marched off to war. Worse yet, the possibility of military conscription loomed, as states ran drafts to fill the ranks of their militias to supply troops for the Union cause. Would men whose consciences forbade participation in war be able to get an exemption from the draft?

Mennonites in Ohio were nervous about this question as the time for the draft approached. Some Mennonites came up with the idea of petitioning President Abraham Lincoln for exemption, and the idea was passed on to John M. Brenneman.

Brenneman (1816-1895) was a Mennonite bishop at Elida, Allen County, Ohio, and a well-respected and well-traveled preacher. His special mission was visiting scattered Mennonites – both small churches and individuals without churches – throughout the west, where they had moved, often for economic opportunity, but without clear, well-organized church support. He had a concern for supporting nonresistance, and was distressed by inconsistencies in the principle's application.

In response to the request for a petition, Brenneman wrote a draft and sent it to Jacob Nold, a Mennonite deacon from Columbiana County, Ohio. Dated August 19, 1862, the petition asked "the President not to consider us too burdensome by presenting to him this, our weak and humble petition, thereby humbly praying and beseeching him to take into consideration our sore distress." He explained that for Mennonites, "it is against their Confession of Faith and also against their conscience to take up arms therewith to destroy human life," but hurried to clarify that "the President must not mistake us to be secessionists or rebels against the government, as we are entirely free from that guilt." He then explained that Mennonites believed in praying for governmental officials, paying taxes, and being submissive to the government

Historical Introduction iii

where this did not conflict with the Word of God. Having laid this foundation, Brenneman presented the request for exemption:

We therefore beseech our good President to favor us in this respect and not allow us to be forced or compelled to take up arms against our consciences, as we would thereby have to renounce our faith and break our promise to God, who alone has power over our consciences...we do by no means expect or ask to be entirely screened from the burden of the war. But we pray and beg for God's sake that the liberty may be granted us to pay a fine when drafted, instead of taking up arms. This privilege has been granted to the Mennonites heretofore, in the United States in time of war...Our Mennonite brethren in Eastern Virginia have been taken by force by the rebels, some of them tied and loaded on wagons, and hauled off to the Rebel Army. But as they would not fight for them upon any conditions they were kept awhile as prisoners, and finally sent home by laying a heavy fine upon them, besides [an additional] two percent [tax] on all their property, as we have been informed. Now we have the confidence in our President and his officers that they are fully as kind and merciful (and we trust much more so) as they of the South.

We would not prescribe to the President how to deal with us. But we humbly pray and beseech him that upon some terms or other we may be allowed our religious liberty. Should it be deemed proper to lay an extra tax upon all of us and our sons as are considered fit subjects for military duties or so much percentage on all their property, we will not murmur or complain at all. We feel that we are dependent creatures: depending on the mercy of God and also upon the mercy of the President and the governors...

We hope and pray that the President will be so kind as to issue immediate orders to the several governors of those states wherein the Mennonites reside, instructing the governors to be favorably inclined to us poor creatures of the dust – especially to the governor of Ohio, as the Mennonites in Ohio seem to be in the most danger.[1]

---

1   John M. Brenneman, Draft of a Petition to Abraham Lincoln, August 19, 1862; printed in *Mennonite Historical Bulletin* 34(4) (October 1973):2-3.

Christianity and War

Having written this draft, Brenneman sent it to Jacob Nold with a cover letter. Brenneman was not convinced that petitioning the President was the best course of action. He exhorted Nold,

> But as I have mentioned before, let us be careful not to put too much confidence in man. Our God is certainly more to be depended on than the President, as he is a Father of mercies and as a father pitieth his children, so God pitieth them that fear him. God has all power in heaven and earth.
> But what is the President? But a poor dying mortal like ourselves, and if we lean entirely upon him for help, I fear we would lean on a broken reed. I do not say that it is entirely wrong to make application to him in such a time of trouble, as Paul also made application to Caesar, when in danger of the Jews. But first of all, let us flee to God who is yet far above the President; yea let us, at the throne of grace, present our petition to God, in true faith, and we are sure of success. But should God be fully determined to chastise us as we have long ago deserved, then we can not escape.[2]

As far as we know, the petition never made it to Lincoln's desk, but exemption for a fee did come. For $200, drafted conscientious objectors in Ohio could be released from service.

Although lukewarm about the idea of petitioning the President, Brenneman was passionate in exhorting nonresistant people to faithfulness and in explaining nonresistant principles to outsiders. Through a series of events in the next year, his now-classic work *Christianity and War* was born.

The chain of events began in May, when Brenneman and Pennsylvania Mennonite minister Peter K. Nissley – who had been on a trip preaching to small western Mennonite communities in Illinois – were stranded in Chicago over Sunday. That morning, Brenneman knocked on the door of John F. Funk, a young Mennonite who was without Mennonite fellowship in the city. He had been befriended by Brenneman the previous fall, when Funk had attended the meeting of Indiana Conference in Elkhart and had taken communion for the first time, with Brenneman presiding.

---

2 August 21, 1862, John M. Brenneman to Jacob Nold; printed in *Mennonite Historical Bulletin* 34(4) (October 1973):3.

Historical Introduction v

Now, Funk and Brenneman together went to Sunday morning worship at Third Presbyterian Church, then, joined by Nissley, went to the Sunday School where Funk was a teacher. The visitors were deeply impressed with the kind of teaching Funk was providing for the city children. Nissley wrote, "I was surprised to hear the word lisped and repeated, as Christ says—Love your enemies, bless them that curse you, do good to them that hate you, and pray for them that despitefully use you and persecute you."[3]

That evening, Brenneman and Funk visited further, and Funk showed Brenneman the partially completed manuscript of a booklet on nonresistance, which he had begun but laid aside. The next day, Funk returned to working on the booklet, probably at Brenneman's encouragement, and on July 22, 1863, he received 1,000 copies of *Warfare: Its Evils, Our Duty* from the printer.

Funk's booklet encouraged nonresistance by appeal to the words of Jesus and by graphic descriptions of the inhumanity of war, led by the "military hero" who "comes to us with garments red with human gore" and "has made himself the greatest murderer of the age, the most extensive robber in all the land."

The tract was all the more remarkable since its author had previously been deeply interested in Republican politics, supported the war effort, and had rather weak convictions for nonresistance. His life had changed, however, after his baptism in Pennsylvania and his first partaking of Communion in Indiana.

Upon seeing the published booklet, Brenneman feared for Funk's personal safety, after publishing such direct words against the war. At Funk's encouragement, however, Brenneman himself picked up his pen and wrote a more extensive booklet on nonresistance. Rather than treating nonresistance as one isolated doctrine to be proven or disproven by Scriptural proof texts, Brenneman put the teaching into a broad context of the Christian life and the kingdom of God. Taking 1 Peter 2:21 as his text, which states that Jesus came "Leaving us an example, that we should follow His

---

3 August 22, 1863, Peter Nissley to John F. Funk; as cited by Joseph Liechty and James O. Lehman, "From Yankee to Nonresistant: John F. Funk's Chicago Years, 1857-1865," *Mennonite Quarterly Review* 59(3) (July 1985):203-247, p. 239.

steps," Brenneman did not immediately answer the question of whether it was right for Christians to go to war. Rather, he began his argument by defining what it means to be a Christian.

According to Brenneman, a true Christian is defined by three characteristics: 1) following the example of Christ, 2) obedience to the teachings of Christ, and 3) being filled with the Spirit of Christ.

Having established these central characteristics of the true Christian, Brenneman then used them to apply a three-point test to involvement in war. Jesus exemplified nonresistance in His personal life, even to the point of death on the cross; this was our example to follow. Jesus taught nonresistance by word in the Sermon on the Mount, and His apostles gave similar teachings; to these, Christians must be obedient. The Spirit of Christ will make us like Him in all things, and that Spirit is one of peace, reconciliation, and love, not of war and killing.

These points make up the core of Brenneman's argument. Other considerations, such as Jesus as the Prince of Peace, the dreadful nature of war (as Funk described in his booklet), the suffering church, etc. were also discussed by Brenneman at fitting points in his work.

With this three-point description of true Christianity, and his application of this definition to nonresistance, Brenneman put nonresistance into a broad and persuasive context which made it integral to and inseparable from the entire Christian life. There was no separation here between faith and works, salvation and action, gospel and ethics. The life of peace, love, and nonresistance is the life of obedience and following Jesus, and the only way of living which is truly spiritual.

To his main argument, Brenneman appended a brief essay titled "An Address to the Mennonite Brethren," pleading for faithfulness in the midst of wartime difficulties and making a case for Mennonites to abstain from party politics. A final brief essay, "A Word to the Careless," used the story of the prophet Jonah as a warning for those who were carelessly sleeping, mindless of their own salvation.

Historical Introduction vii

By August 1863, the manuscript was in Funk's hands, and 2,000 copies were printed by October. The book was officially anonymous, probably due to the author's apprehension due to the hostility of local patriots and also possibly from motives of humility. During Brenneman's lifetime, the book's title page never carried his name, even when reprinted after the war.

Both books sold well. Funk's book sold out and was reprinted by Canadian Mennonites in 1864. In that year, Brenneman's was printed in German, in which language it was reprinted in 1868. Also in 1868, the English edition was reprinted with some modifications; most notably, the essay "A Word to the Careless" was omitted. In 1915, the 1868 edition was reprinted in Arthur, Illinois; this edition was again reprinted in 1990 in Crofton, Kentucky. These versions were the first to print Brenneman's name on the title page. The 1863 edition was also reprinted as an appendix to *Mennonites of the Ohio and Eastern Conference*, by Grant M. Stoltzfus (1969).

The present edition presents the text from the 1868 edition, with the addition of the 1863 essay "A Word to the Careless." Funk's booklet is also included as an appendix. A few slight modifications to punctuation and spelling have been made where necessary. All subheadings, illustrations, and verse reference footnotes are the present publisher's additions. Unsigned footnotes are Brenneman's.

We present this book to the public, not as an academic or intellectual exercise, but for the edification of the church and in the hope that the reader will be strengthened and confirmed in a conviction for nonresistance, and will come away with a vision of Christianity in which salvation and nonresistance are parts of an inseparable whole.

Andrew V. Ste. Marie
June 2, 2017

Original Preface

Whereas the so-called Mennonites have always been conscientiously opposed to wars and blood-shed of all kinds, for which they have been looked upon by some with scorn, hatred, and contempt, as though they were a people that should scarcely be tolerated under a civil government, the writer has been induced, in the following work, to give and set forth some of the principal grounds and reasons from the Holy Scriptures, showing, why it is that the Mennonites believe in a "defenseless" Christianity, and why it is that they cannot feel justified in the sight of God, to take up arms to slay their enemies. It is sincerely hoped that, after a careful perusal of the following remarks, the unprejudiced reader will, at least, be somewhat more favorably inclined toward the Mennonites, and feel convinced that it is not without many strong and cogent Scriptural reasons and arguments in their favor, that, concerning war in all its forms, they differ in their sentiments from many others.

These remarks have not been written with any intention to condemn those who differ from us in the faith and practice of their religion, but merely to show forth our grounds and reasons for believing as we do; and, if others have more light on this subject, and feel clear in their consciences to go and slay their enemies, we will freely leave that between them and their God to decide; and could the writer of this little work be convinced, from the doctrines of Christ and His apostles that he is in error, he feels willing to lay aside the sentiments which he now holds, and to accept those that are better; and, inasmuch as he is an uneducated man he hopes that the kind Christian reader will freely overlook all errors into which he may have fallen in the preparation of this work; and if by the blessing of God, it may be the means, and have the tendency, to induce many to examine the Scriptures more closely, and happily bring some from error's ways, strengthen and encourage Christians, and make them more vigorous in the path of Christian duty—then the writer will feel that his feeble efforts have not been altogether fruitless. May God give enlightened eyes, to every reader.

Christianity and War Considered, Illustrated and Set Forth

Leaving us an example, that we should follow His steps.
1 Pet. 2:21.

These words of our text were written by that highly inspired apostle, Peter, in a time when Christians had to endure great persecution, and suffer great afflictions, to ENCOURAGE them, "in patience to possess their souls."[4] This seems to have been one of the main objects of the apostle throughout this epistle, as we may clearly see in the following passages: "But, and if ye suffer for righteousness' sake, happy are ye; and be not afraid of their terror, neither be ye troubled." 1 Pet. 3:14. "For it is better, if the will of God be so, that ye suffer for well-doing, than for evil-doing: for Christ also hath once suffered for sins, the just for the unjust, that He might bring us to God." Vs. 17, 18. "Forasmuch, then, as Christ hath suffered for us in the flesh, arm yourselves likewise with the same mind; for he that hath suffered in the flesh hath ceased from sin." Chap. 4:1. "Though now for a season, if need be, ye are in heaviness through manifold temptations; that the trial of your faith, being much more precious than of gold that perisheth, though it be tried with fire, might be found unto praise, and honor, and glory at the appearing of Jesus Christ." Chap. 1:6, 7. "Beloved, think it not strange concerning the fiery trial which is to try you, as though some strange thing happened unto you: but rejoice, inasmuch as ye are partakers of Christ's sufferings; that when His glory shall be revealed, ye may be glad also with exceeding joy. If ye be reproached for the name of Christ, happy

---
4   Luke 21:19.

are ye; for the Spirit of glory and of God resteth upon you." Chap. 4:12-14. "Be sober, be vigilant; because your adversary, the devil, as a roaring lion, walketh about, seeking whom he may devour; whom resist steadfast in the faith, knowing that the same afflictions are accomplished in your brethren that are in the world. But the God of all grace, who hath called us unto His eternal glory by Christ Jesus, after that ye have suffered a while, make you perfect, establish, strengthen, settle you." Chap. 5:8-10. "For this is thankworthy, if a man for conscience toward God endure grief, suffering wrongfully. For what glory is it, if, when ye be buffeted for your faults, ye shall take it patiently, but if, when ye do well, and suffer for it, ye take it patiently, THIS is acceptable with God." Chap. 2:19, 20. "But let none of you suffer as a murderer, or as a thief, or as an evil-doer, or as a busy-body in other men's matters. Yet, if any man suffer as a Christian, let him not be ashamed; but let him glorify God on this behalf." Chap. 4:15, 16. "Let them that suffer according to the will of God, commit the keeping of their souls to Him in well-doing, as unto a faithful Creator." V. 19.

A Suffering People

By searching the Scriptures and the history of the churches, we shall find that God's people have always been a suffering people, from righteous Abel down to the present time. Moses "chose rather to suffer affliction with the people of God than to enjoy the pleasures of sin for a season."—Yea, David says, "Many are the afflictions of the righteous;" and Paul declares, "For unto you it is given in the behalf of Christ, not only to believe on Him, but also to suffer for His sake." And take, my brethren, as another example of suffering, affliction, and patience, the prophets. Yea, suffering and affliction seems to be the lot of God's people upon the earth; as Peter says in the verse of which our text is a part: "For even hereunto were ye called, because Christ also suffered for us, leaving us an example, that we should follow His steps."

We find nothing in all this epistle, commanding, directing, or enjoining, or exhorting, or advising, or in any way recommending, or even yet allowing, or indicating in the remotest sense, the idea that these suffering Christians might resent the persecutions,

Christianity and War 3

Why must Christians suffer for righteousness' sake?

and sufferings and afflictions, which were thus laid upon them; or that they might defend themselves against their enemies, or that they might rise up in arms and repel and destroy their persecutors; but rather the reverse, by setting forth Christ as an example of suffering; who, when he was reviled, reviled not again; when he suffered, he threatened not; but committed himself to Him that judgeth righteously; and if they thus suffered as Christians, they need not be ashamed.

But why is it that Christians must thus suffer? Surely, it is not for any evil that they have done, but "for righteousness' sake"; as righteous Abel had to suffer because his works were righteous and his brother's evil. Because they "are not of this world," and stand aloof from all its wicked practices, therefore the "world hateth them"; for light and darkness have no communion with each other, and Christians have no fellowship with the unfruitful works of darkness, but rather reprove them; therefore they must suffer of the children of darkness. Because the difference between the children of God and the children of the devil is so great that the one can have no part, no agreement with the other, Christians can never unite with the children of sin, nor take part with them in their evil works; therefore again, must they suffer the reproaches of the children of sin. Such has always been the case since sin entered into the world.

May a Christian Fight?

Now, whereas the present time is a time of war and bloodshed, the question has frequently been asked, "May a Christian also take a part in this work of violence and bloodshed? Or, may a Christian take up the weapons of death, go forth to war, and destroy the lives of his enemies; and at the same time obey the gospel of Jesus Christ, and be justifiable in the sight of God?" That this is surely, a fair and reasonable question, all must admit; and of so great importance, that it demands the most serious consideration of all who profess to be Christians. To answer this question is my present design; but before I proceed, I will first endeavor to show the origin and import of the name Christian, and what is it to be a Christian; after which the question may be more readily answered.

What is a Christian?

The first followers of Christ were, by their enemies, called Galileans, Nazarenes and other names of contempt. Among themselves they were called Saints, from their holiness; Believers, from their believing in Christ as the Messiah; Brethren, from their mutual love, and their close relation to God and to each other; and Disciples (signifying scholars or learners), from their learning their religion from Christ as their teacher.

By nature men are sinners, and not Christians—children of wrath—dead in trespasses and sins—ignorant and estranged from the life of God, and without God in the world; and consequently in a lost, and most deplorable condition. Christ came into the world to save sinners from this lost and miserable condition: but before He can or will save them they must be convinced that they are lost and, like the prodigal son, in a perishing condition. They must come to a knowledge of the truth, to a knowledge of sin, which is by the law; which condemns them for its violation. This knowledge of sin and condemnation makes them feel poor in spirit; yea, it makes them feel that they are wretched, miserable, poor, blind, and naked; it makes them feel that they are lost sinners indeed; and this again brings them to feel sorrow and penitence, and to mourn over their sins, which becomes as a burden to them, too heavy to be borne—like David of old, they are "bowed down greatly, they go mourning all the day long"[5]—like the jailor at Philippi, they will be brought to cry out, "What must I do to be saved?"[6] Such sin-sick, burdened, and heavy-laden souls Christ calls to Him, saying, "Come unto me all ye that labor and are heavy laden, and I will give you rest: take my yoke upon you, and learn of me; for I am meek and lowly in heart: and ye shall find rest unto your souls." Matt. 11:28, 29.

Christ is a teacher come from God, to teach men the doctrine of salvation. "He taught as one having authority;"[7] and hence, poor, heavy-laden sinners must come to Him and learn of Him the words of eternal life, the words of salvation and reconciliation—must learn to do well, learn righteousness; yea, learn Christ.

To learn also signifies to imitate; therefore penitent sinners must imitate Christ by walking in His steps. Those thus learning, as remarked above, in the days of Christ, were called disciples, because they came to Him for instruction. Jesus said unto those Jews which believed on Him, "If ye continue in My word, then are ye My disciples indeed." Jn. 8:31. Again: "By this shall all men know that ye are My disciples if ye have love one to another." 13:35. The conditions of discipleship with Christ are plainly expressed in the following passage: "Whosoever he be, that forsaketh not all that he hath, he cannot be My disciple;"[8] for the "disciple is not above his master."[9] A true disciple must, then, be one who learns of Christ, one who is a faithful and obedient follower of Christ, bearing his cross after him; yea, one who follows his steps through

---

5 Psalm 38:6.
6 Acts 16:30.
7 Matthew 7:29.
8 Luke 14:33.
9 Matthew 10:24; Luke 6:40.

evil as well as through good report; one who has renounced sin and Satan and all that is contrary to God's holy will; and who as a poor, lost sinner has delivered himself up to Jesus, to be his, to learn of him, and to serve him all the days of his life. To him there is nothing so near, or so dear in all the world that he is not willing to forsake it for Christ's sake, if it stands between him and his Savior; knowing that without renouncing and forsaking all that is contrary to his Master's will, he cannot be his disciple.

Such disciples, we find, "were called Christians, first in Antioch." Acts 11:26. Agrippa said to Paul, "Almost thou persuadest me to be a Christian;"[10] and Peter said, "If any man suffer as a Christian, let him not be ashamed."[11] Thus, it seems, it became the general name of the disciples, in the days of the apostles, originating from Christ, just as the name Lutheran originated from Luther, or Calvinist from Calvin, or Mennonite from Menno.

But, surely, to be a Christian in reality, signifies more than bearing merely the outward name; and to be a Christian indeed, is of a thousand times more value, than to be merely called a Christian, without possessing what the name implies; although it is used at this day as a general name; first, in contradistinction to Pagans, Mahometans,[12] and Jews; secondly, to denote the open professor of Christianity in contradistinction to those who are not professors. The name, when first given, was very appropriately applied; as the name Gentile was odious to the Jews, and the name Jew was odious to the Gentiles; the name Christian swallowed up both in one common and agreeable appellation. Paul says, "As many as have been baptized into Christ, have put on Christ; there is neither Jew nor Greek, there is neither bond nor free, for ye are all one in Christ Jesus."[13] Therefore, it was also proper that their name should be one; but as all are not Israelites indeed who bear the name, so all are not Christians who are called by that name: to be only called a Christian will never benefit us in the least if we have not what the name signifies.

---

10 Acts 26:28.
11 1 Peter 4:16.
12 Muslims.—*Ed.*
13 Galatians 3:27-28.

Christians Are Anointed

Now, as before remarked, the name Christian was derived from Christ, which signifies anointed; as anointed is the English translation of the Greek name Christ, and of the Hebrew, Messiah. Jesus is frequently called the "Anointed." "The Spirit of the Lord God is upon me, because the Lord hath anointed me to preach good tidings to the meek," &c. Is. 61:1. These words Christ applies to himself. Lu. 4:18, 21. God anointed Jesus of Nazareth "with the Holy Ghost and with power." Acts 4:27, and 10:38. "He was anointed with the oil of gladness above His fellows." Heb. 1:9. God commanded Moses to make a "holy anointing oil", and "anoint Aaron and his sons, and consecrate them." Ex. 30:23, 25, 30. "And he poured of the anointing oil on Aaron's head and anointed him to sanctify him." Lev. 8:12. Of this anointing the psalmist speaks thus: "Behold, how good and how pleasant it is for brethren to dwell together in unity;" as undoubtedly all do that are anointed by the Spirit; "it is like the precious ointment upon the head, that ran down upon the beard, even Aaron's beard, that went down to the skirts of his garments." Ps. 133:1, 2. Aaron, being thus anointed, was a striking type of Christ; the holy anointing oil being so plentifully poured upon his head, that it ran down over his beard and the skirts of his garments: so Jesus received the Spirit, not by measure, but, according to the common expression, above measure; and as the oil ran down over Aaron, we may reasonably conjecture that his members, namely, his eyes, ears, mouth, &c., his hands and feet also, received more or less of the same anointing. His head, however, received the greater portion, and as Christ is the head of his followers, who are called his members, they must certainly also (as Christ, the head, is so plentifully anointed) be anointed with the same anointing, although in a much smaller portion. Of this anointing, the Apostle Paul makes mention as follows: "Now he which establisheth us

> To be only called a Christian will never benefit us in the least if we have not what the name signifies.

with you in Christ, and hath anointed us, is God; who hath also sealed us, and given the earnest of the Spirit in our hearts." 2 Cor. 1:21, 22. John says, "Ye have an unction from the Holy One, and know all things." Jn. 2:20. And again, "The anointing which ye have received of Him abideth in you, and ye need not that any man teach you; but as the same anointing teacheth you of all things" (v. 27); and as the name of Christ signifies anointed, it is evident and beyond dispute, that the name Christian, which is derived from it, must signify the same; for "if any man have not the Spirit of Christ, he is none of His" (Rom. 8:9), and consequently is no Christian.

The course of becoming a Christian, and the substance of a true Christian life, are the same as that of a true disciple, as already set forth; yet, to make the matter plain, and to give the true import of the name Christian, I will use another, and a different illustration, which will, however, agree with that already given.

First, a true Christian, then, is one who has been convinced of his lost and sinful condition, one who has seen his unholiness, and thus, with a penitent and contrite heart, fled to Jesus for refuge, praying, like David, for a clean heart and a new spirit; or, like the leper, saying, "Lord, if Thou wilt Thou canst make me clean"[14]: thus confidently trusting in him as the only true Savior, with a determination to adhere to him and to become his disciple; like Jacob of old, saying, "I will not let thee go, until thou bless me; and thus cleaving unto the Lord, he became one spirit with Him."[15]

Secondly, a Christian, then, is one who stands in very close connection with Christ: even so closely connected with Him as the branch is with the vine, as Christ also says, "I am the vine, ye are the branches."[16] "He that abideth in Me and I in him, the same bringeth forth much fruit."[17] Now as the branch is connected with the vine, and receives from it life, and spirit, and nourishment, and becomes fruitful, and also partakes of the same nature with the vine: so Christians are living and fruitful branches of Christ: and

---

14 Matthew 8:2; Mark 1:40; Luke 5:12.
15 According to Luther's translation.
16 John 15:5a.
17 John 15:5b.

Christianity and War 9

as they are partakers of his life, his Spirit, and his holy nature, it is very evident that they must also bring forth the fruits of the Spirit, which are "love, joy, peace, long-suffering, gentleness, goodness, faith, meekness, temperance." Gal. 5:22, 23.

Now, he that bringeth not forth the fruits of the Spirit, cannot have the Spirit, for the Spirit is always fruitful; and he that hath not the Spirit of Christ, is none of his, and consequently can be no Christian, no matter by what name he is called; for to be a Christian without being a partaker with Christ of the Holy Spirit, is an utter impossibility. Paul says, "Now we have received, not the spirit of the world, but the Spirit which is of God." 1 Cor. 2:12. And again, "God has not given us the spirit of fear; but of power, and of love, and of a sound mind." 2 Tim. 1:7. "Because ye are sons, God hath sent forth the Spirit of his Son into your hearts, crying Abba, Father." Gal. 4:6.—"The love of God is shed abroad in our hearts by the Holy Ghost which is given unto us." Rom. 5:5. Hence, we may plainly see that a Christian is influenced by, and also a partaker of, the Holy Spirit; and how could it be otherwise? for he is a branch of Christ the true vine, a member of his body, flesh of his flesh, and bone of his bone: and, as Christ was so richly anointed, it is evident that his members must likewise partake of the same, which makes them partakers of his holy nature and of his mind. Paul says, "Now we have the mind of Christ;" and again, "Let this mind be in you, which was also in Christ Jesus."

Thirdly, to be a true Christian, is to be like Christ, in nature, practice, walk and conversation—to imitate him by walking in his footsteps. Was Christ meek and lowly in heart? So is the Christian. Was Christ good and kind, merciful, amiable, benevolent, and friendly to all mankind, even to his bitterest enemies? So is the Christian. Was Christ harmless, and of a lamb-like disposition? So is the Christian. Did Christ love his enemies and pray for them? So will the Christian. In fact, all the holy virtues and dispositions of Christ will be, to a greater or less degree, the leading principles and features of a Christian's life. "Christ liveth in the Christian" (Gal. 2:20)—yea, the life of Christ is the Christian's LIFE, as Paul writes to the Colossians, "When Christ, WHO IS OUR LIFE, shall appear, then shall ye also appear with him in glory." Col. 3:4.

How, then, can a Christian live a life contrary to the principles and virtues of Christ, if Christ is formed and lives in him? Gal. 4:19. Would not then Christ be against himself? But his life in the Christian is of the same nature and the same disposition, as the life manifested in himself: it changes not, but still remains the same, "yesterday, to-day, and forever."[18] A Christian thus imitates Christ, from whom the name is derived: being "changed into the same image, from glory to glory, even as by the Spirit of the Lord." 2 Cor. 3:18. "Conformed to the image of God's Son,"[19] he follows in his steps, is in possession of his Spirit and temper, and lives as He lived in the world. The foregoing remarks are very aptly illustrated by the following incident. Alexander the Great had a soldier in his army whose name was likewise Alexander; but who, unlike his namesake, was a great coward. "Either be like me," said Alexander, "or lay aside my name." So it should be with us who bear the name of Christ. Oh, how self-contradicting it is to be called a Christian, while engaged in serving the devil, and doing his work!

Fourthly, to be a true Christian, we must depart from iniquity: to this the name obliges us. Without doing this we have no right, no claim, to the sacred name. "Let everyone that nameth the name of Christ, depart from iniquity;" that is, either let him depart from iniquity, or else never dare to assume that holy name.

Fifthly, to be a Christian, is to deny ourselves, to take up our cross, and to follow Christ; as he has left us "an example, that we should follow his steps." Now, to follow in the steps of anyone, surely requires close observation, close imitation. It requires to be found walking in the same path. "The steps of a good man are ordered by the Lord." Ps. 37:23. "Because he prays the Lord to order

---

18 Hebrews 13:8.
19 Romans 8:29.

his steps." 119:113. "Walked we not in the same spirit? walked we not in the same steps?" 2 Cor. 12:18.

Sixthly, to be a Christian implies, first, that we have passed from death unto life, from darkness into light, from the power and influence of Satan unto God. Secondly, it implies a new birth, a renewing of the mind, a regeneration of the soul, a change from an earthly and carnal to heavenly and spiritual mind. Thirdly, it "implies a child and an heir of God,"[20] whose "conversation is in heaven"[21]—who seeks an inheritance which is "incorruptible and undefiled, and that fadeth not away, reserved in heaven"[22]—who looks for "a city which hath foundations whose builder and maker is God." Heb. 11:10.

Can a Christian Fight?

And now comes the all-important question to be answered, namely, Can a Christian take up the weapons of death, go forth to war, and destroy the lives of his enemies, and at the same time obey the gospel of Jesus Christ, and be justifiable in the sight of God?

This question I will now endeavor to answer; not by my own knowledge and wisdom, not by the views and opinions of men, nor by "cunningly devised fables;"[23] but by the pure doctrines and the example of Jesus Christ and his apostles; and, certainly, no one who professes to be a Christian, will dare dispute these.

Christ is that Prophet of whom Moses spoke, saying, "The Lord thy God will raise up unto thee a Prophet, from the midst of thy brethren, like unto me; unto Him ye shall hearken. . . . And it shall come to pass, that whosoever will not hearken unto my words, which he shall speak in my name, I will require it of him." Deut. 18:15, 19.

The above passage Peter applies as follows: "For Moses truly said unto the fathers, A Prophet shall the Lord your God raise up unto you, of your brethren, like unto me; him shall ye hear in all

---

20   cf. Galatians 4:7.
21   Philippians 3:20.
22   1 Peter 1:4.
23   2 Peter 1:16.

12 Christianity and War

A Christian who does not love Jesus is like a fire that gives no heat.

things, whatsoever he shall say unto you: and it shall come to pass, that every soul which will not hear that Prophet, shall be destroyed from among the people." Acts 3:22, 23. God himself, by a voice out of a cloud from heaven, declared saying, "This is My beloved Son in whom I am well pleased: hear ye him" (Matt. 17:5); and as every soul which will not hear that Prophet, is threatened with destruction, surely his words must be of great authority and weight. Christ himself says, "Ye are My friends, if ye do whatsoever I command you." Jn. 15:14. These words evidently imply that, if we do not what he commands us, we are his enemies: "and those mine enemies," he will finally say, "which would not that I should reign over them, bring hither, and slay them before me." Lu. 19:27. Again, he says, "If a man love me, he will keep my words": to the Jews he said, "If God were your Father, ye would love me."[24] Thus a Christian, without loving Jesus, would be like a fire giving no heat.

---

24 John 8:42.

The Words of Jesus

Now, Jesus in his Sermon on the Mount, said, "Ye have heard that it hath been said, An eye for an eye, and a tooth for a tooth"— this was recompensing evil for evil, which the apostle strictly forbids—"but I say unto you that ye resist not evil."[25] Now what mean these words of Christ and Paul? Surely they must mean something: they were not spoken or written in vain, or for nought; and is this not their plain and simple meaning, namely, that, if a man does an evil to us of any kind out of ill-will, we shall not resist that evil by returning evil to him again, but rather suffer him to repeat the same evil unto us a second time?—as the second clause of the foregoing verse explains: "Whosoever shall smite thee on thy right cheek, turn to him the other also; and if any man will sue thee at the law, and take away thy coat, let him have thy cloak also."[26] Or, according to Luther, If a man should sue thee at the law, rather than have a law-suit with him, let him have thy cloak also, if by so doing thou canst avoid the suit; and not say like the worldly minded, "I will spend all that I have, before I will give up to him." How many times do we see men spend, at law, a hundred dollars to gain five or ten dollars—the gainer at law very often being the loser in money very largely, and this simply in order to have revenge: but Paul says, "Now, there is utterly a fault among you, because ye go to law one with another. Why do ye not rather take wrong? Why do ye not rather suffer yourselves to be defrauded?" 1 Cor. 6:7. A true Christian will rather take wrong, and suffer wrong, than go to law—he will rather give more than is just in order that he may avoid a lawsuit.

Our great Prophet goes on in his discourse, saying, "Ye have heard that it hath been said, Thou shalt love thy neighbor and hate thine enemy; but I say unto you, Love your enemies, bless them that curse you, do good to them that hate you, and pray for them which despitefully use you, and persecute you."[27] Who is it that says these things? It is Christ, the Lord from heaven, "who is Lord

---

25 Matthew 5:39.
26 Matthew 5:40.
27 Matthew 5:43-44.

of all"[28]: it is that great Prophet, whom we are commanded to hear in all things, on pain of being destroyed: it is Christ, "the Amen, the faithful and true Witness, the beginning of the creation of God" (Rev. 3:14), "by whom God made the worlds, and by whom he spoke unto us in these last days" (Heb. 1:2): it is Christ, who "spoke as never man spoke"[29]: it is Christ, before whose judgment seat we must all appear. Therefore, "see that ye refuse not him that speaketh; for, if they escaped not who refused him who spoke on earth, much more shall not we escape, if we turn away from him who speaketh from heaven." Heb. 12:25. This is that Christ, that great Prophet, who says, "Love your enemies." This is a positive command, which a Christian must obey; for there can be no such thing as a disobedient Christian: this would be a contradiction of terms; "for the disobedient shall be punished with an everlasting destruction." 2 Thess. 1:8, 9. "The wrath of God cometh on the children of disobedience." Col. 3:9. The worldly-minded are perhaps ready to say, "These are hard sayings, who can hear them?" but they are nevertheless true sayings; for they are the very words of that great Prophet whom we are to hear, or be destroyed—Christ, from whom we received the Christian name, and of whose nature Christians are partakers—Christ, who loved his enemies and died for them. Rom. 5:10. How, then, can a Christian hate his enemy, and follow in the steps of Christ? Or, how can he hate his enemy, and still be a living member of Christ? For, says Christ, "If ye love them which love you, what is your reward? Do not even the publicans" (who are not Christians) "the same?"[30] But Paul says, "If thine enemy hunger, feed him; if he thirst, give him drink: for in so doing thou shalt heap coals of fire on his head." Rom. 12:20. And now, I would ask this most solemn question, If a man love his

> **There can be no such thing as a disobedient Christian: this would be a contradiction of terms!**

---

28   Acts 10:36.
29   John 7:46.
30   Matthew 5:46.

enemy, can he destroy his life and his property? make his wife a widow, his children orphans? Christ also commands us to love our neighbor as ourselves, and teaches us that ALL MEN with whom we may come in contact, are to be considered our neighbors, as is clearly shown in the parable given in Luke 10:29, 37. And again, "Whatsoever ye would that men should do to you, do ye even so to them."[31] Now, we certainly would not wish our neighbor to come and to destroy OUR life and OUR property, but would desire him to leave us undisturbed and unharmed: go thou, then, and do likewise.

To "love our enemies," is a positive command, wherein Christ has also "left us an example that we should follow His steps." The ungodly cannot love their enemies, neither can they follow Christ's steps; but to love their enemies is the characteristic of all true Christians. The next command in the verse under consideration is, "Bless them that curse you." But how, someone may say, can we bless them that curse us? I answer, Just as Jacob blessed his angry brother, Esau, when on his journey, returning to his fatherland. He heard that Esau was coming to meet him with 400 men; and, fearing that Esau intended to do him harm, he prepared a great gift, and sent it to Esau: and, as he approached him, Jacob bowed down before him to the ground seven times; "and Esau ran to meet him, and embraced him, and fell on his neck, and kissed him; and they wept."[32] And Esau said to Jacob, "What meanest thou by all this drove which I met?" And he said, "These are to find grace in the sight of my Lord;"[33] but Esau declined to take the gift. But Jacob said, "Take, I pray thee, my blessing that is brought to thee."[34] Thus Jacob blessed his brother with a gift, and by so doing, heaped coals of fire on his head, which so melted him that he became as a lamb before his brother. Thus we must overcome evil with good. Thus Joseph also blessed his brethren, who had sold him into Egypt. Peter says, "Not rendering evil for evil, or railing for railing, but contrariwise, a blessing."[35]

---

31 Matthew 7:12.
32 Genesis 33:4.
33 Genesis 33:8.
34 Genesis 33:11.
35 1 Peter 3:9.

Christians should do good to the bodies, the families, and the souls of those who hate them.

Do them good in any and in every way they can!

The next command in the verse is, "Do good to them that hate you." The Apostle Paul bids us "do good unto all men,"[36] which includes those also that hate us. It is wicked to hate anyone, therefore Christians should not be like those that hate them; but contrariwise, do them good—do good to their bodies, to their families, to their souls. Do them good in any and in every way they can. In this way, we may appease and overcome their hatred, as Jacob did that of Esau. The manner of Christian professors generally is, not only not to do good to those that cherish hatred toward them, but to hate them likewise in return, and to do them all the evil they can besides; but this is contrary to the teachings of Christ, contrary to the spirit of the gospel, and in direct opposition to the example of Christ; for in this also Christ "left us an example, that we should follow his steps."

We must also pray for those who "despitefully use us, and persecute us." Now, no man can pray in sincerity for his persecutors, while at the same time he is aiming to take their lives: such a prayer is an open mockery in the sight of God. Stephen, the first Christian martyr, when his persecutors were stoning him to death, kneeled down and cried with a loud voice, saying, "Lord, lay not this sin to their charge."[37] Christ, in his bitterest agony on the cross, cried, "Father, forgive them, for they know not what

---

36 Galatians 6:10.
37 Acts 7:60.

they do;"[38] thus in this also "leaving us an example, that we should follow his steps."

The Spirit of Christ

These foregoing commandments we must fulfill, if we would be the "children of our Father which is in heaven;"[39] and, in doing and fulfilling these commandments, we prove, and make it manifest, that we are God's children; "and, if children, then heirs: heirs of God and joint-heirs with Christ." Rom. 8:17. But on the other hand, those who hate their enemies, curse those that curse them, do evil to those that hate them, and pray not for those that despitefully use and persecute them, prove and make it manifest, that they are the children of their father, the devil; as Christ said to those disobedient Jews, "And the lusts of your father ye will do: he was a murderer from the beginning." John 8:44. When Christ sent messengers before his face, and they entered into a village of the Samaritans to make ready for him, and the Samaritans did not receive him; James and John, when they saw it, were so enraged, that they said, "Lord, wilt thou that we command fire to come down from heaven and consume them, even as Elias did?" But Jesus turned and rebuked them, saying, "Ye know not what manner of spirit ye are of"—or, according to Luther, "Know ye not what spirit's children ye are?"—"for the Son of Man is not come to destroy men's lives, but to save them." Lu. 9:52-56.

How ready were James and John to avenge themselves of this affront to their Master, by commanding fire to come down from heaven to consume those who had offered it! This was still the manifestation, in their hearts, of old Adam, the natural man, the unregenerate heart. But Christ taught them a different lesson. Instead of calling down fire and vengeance upon those who despitefully use us, we must call down grace and forgiveness upon them. "Father, forgive them,"[40] was the prayer of Christ. He did not destroy men's lives, when persecuted and abused by them, and, therefore, neither have his followers any right to do it. Here-

---

38   Luke 23:34.
39   Matthew 5:45.
40   Luke 23:34.

in Christ has also "left us an example, that we should follow his steps."

Surely, then, if Christians are members of Christ, and branches of him, the true vine, yea, possessors of his Spirit, and anointed with the same, they cannot be engaged in destroying men's lives and property, and at the same time have in their hearts the love of Christ. Now, it seems, the Jews were well aware of the fact, that Christ taught a non-resistant doctrine, when they said, "If we let him thus alone, all men will believe on him, and the Romans shall come, and take away our place and nation." Jn. 11:48. Jesus said to Pilate, "My kingdom is not of this world: if my kingdom were of this world, then would my servants fight, that I should not be delivered to the Jews; but now is my kingdom not from hence." Jn. 18:36. This seems to have been the reason—because his kingdom was not of this world—that his servants would not fight; and if they would not fight then, why should they now? although Peter, it seems, was quite ready to fight for his Master, when he drew his sword, and cut off the ear of the high priest's servant. He was not yet fully acquainted with the nature of Christ's kingdom; but here again Christ sharply rebuked him, saying, "Put up again thy sword into his place: for all they that take the sword, shall perish with the sword" (Matt. 26:52); and Jesus, in order to "leave us an example that we should follow his steps," touched the servant's ear and healed him. Luke 22:51.

But how can this be so, that all who "take the sword shall perish with the sword," since many take the sword and go forth and slay their enemies, and yet do not perish thereby? This is very true, but there is yet another sword, even the word of God, which is called a sword, and by that sword shall men be judged at the last day; so that by taking the carnal sword to slay their enemies, contrary to Christ's teaching, men put themselves in danger of perishing by the spiritual sword, or the sword of Christ's mouth; for he says, "Repent, or else I will come unto thee quickly, and will fight against them with the sword of my mouth." Rev. 2:16. Again, "He that killeth with the sword, must be killed with the sword. Here is the patience and the faith of the saints." Rev. 13:10. Mark, "he *must* be killed with the sword." The sentence will be pronounced

Christianity and War

Like thousands of other saints, the Apostle James was killed with the sword.

against him by the sword of Christ's mouth, "Depart from me, ye cursed, into everlasting fire, prepared for the devil and his angels" (Matt. 20:41); which is synonymous to "the lake which burneth with fire and brimstone," in which the unbelievers shall have their part, "which is the second death." Rev. 21:3. "Here is the patience and the faith of the saints."[41] The Savior admonished his followers, "in patience to possess their souls."[42] Christians are also called "saints." A saint signifies a holy one, because he has been anointed, consecrated, and set apart for a holy use. Many thousands of holy saints have also been killed with the sword, who were strengthened and blessed with faith and patience to endure their trial, even to the end. But as Christ's kingdom is not of this world, it must be of the world beyond this, of the spiritual, the heavenly world, and therefore a spiritual and heavenly kingdom,

---

41 Revelation 13:10.
42 Luke 21:19.

which has its beginning within in the Christian. And as Christ is a Prince of peace, his kingdom also must be a kingdom of peace.

Peace

When Christ, the Prince of peace, was born in Bethlehem, a multitude of the heavenly host came down from heaven proclaiming "peace on earth, and good will to men." Luke 2:14. Christ came and preached "peace to them that were afar off and to them that were nigh." Ep. 2:17. God sent his word unto the children of Israel, preaching "peace by Jesus Christ." Acts 10:36. Jesus said unto his disciples, "Peace I leave with you, my peace I give unto you, not as the world giveth, give I unto you." Jn. 14:27. His gospel is called the "gospel of peace." Ep. 6:15. He himself is the "Author of peace." 1 Cor. 14:33. "The fruit of the Spirit is peace" (Gal. 5:22), wherewith his children are anointed. "Christ is our peace." Ep. 2:14. Paul says, "Let the peace of God rule in your hearts." Col. 3:15. Christians are commanded to follow peace with all men: "If it be possible, as much as lieth in you, live peaceably with all men." Rom. 12:18. "The fruit of righteousness is sown in peace of them that make peace." Jas. 3:18. "Blessed are the peacemakers; for they shall be called the children of God." Matt. 5:9. How, then, shall they make war? If the peacemakers are the children of God, then peacebreakers must be the children of the devil. If Christ is a King of peace, then his subjects, or the members which compose his kingdom, must be peaceful, too. In this peaceful kingdom, then, there can be no war, no fighting, no quarreling; neither can there be hatred, envyings, and strife, or bloodshed; for where envyings and strife are, there is confusion and every evil work, which, James says, "is not the wisdom from above; but is earthly, sensual, devilish." Jas. 3:15. Jude speaks of some who are sensual, having not the Spirit. Jud. 19. Now, where such earthly, sensual, and devilish principles are manifested and practiced, there can be no Christianity; for, "the wisdom which is from above is first pure, then peaceable, gentle, and easy to be entreated, full of mercy and good fruits, without partiality, and without hypocrisy." James 3:17.

Christians can never make war, as the Spirit by which they are led and influenced, is a spirit of peace and love: yea, the very essence of Christianity is love and peace, and according to Christ's doctrine, a Christian will do to others as he would wish them to do to him. He will do no harm, nor any wrong to anyone, but rather suffer wrong himself, for which he needs not be ashamed; as Christ has also suffered wrongfully, "leaving us an example, that

The nature of a lamb is well known to all: when it sees the wolf coming, it will flee.

we should follow His steps," "who did not sin, neither was guile found in his mouth,"[43] and "who was led as a lamb to the slaughter, and as a sheep before her shearers is dumb, so he opened not his mouth." Isa. 53:7. His followers are also called lambs, because they have imbibed the spirit, nature, and disposition of Christ. Christ said to his disciples, "Behold, I send you forth as lambs among wolves." Lu. 10:3. Again, Christ said to Peter, "Feed My lambs." Jn. 21:15. What harmless and defenseless creatures are lambs! Like them, Christians ought also to be "harmless, the sons of God, without rebuke, in the midst of a crooked and perverse

---

43   1 Peter 2:22.

nation, among whom they shine as lights in the world."[44] They must be "harmless as doves." Matt. 10:16. Christ, who left them such a bright example, was harmless, undefiled, and separate from sinners. The nature of a lamb is well known to all: when it sees the wolf coming, it will flee. Christians, when persecuted in one city, are commanded to flee to another, as it is not in their nature to bite and devour their wolfish persecutors. Paul says, "Dearly beloved, avenge not yourselves, but rather give place unto wrath: for it is written, Vengeance is mine; I will repay, saith the Lord." Rom. 12:19. How, then, shall we give place unto wrath? I answer, If a man meets you in wrath, enraged and embittered against you, give place, make room, resist not the evil he offers you with evil again; be like a lamb, as Christ has left us an example. He reviled not, when he was reviled; he threatened not, when he suffered; "but committed himself to him that judgeth righteously:" so Christians must commit themselves to him to whom vengeance belongs. He is "Judge of all the earth."[45] He will certainly do right. What a wonderful sight it would be, to see a flock of harmless lambs, meeting a pack of ravenous wolves, tear and devour them! Could a man believe his own eyes, if he saw such a sight? Or, if he should tell his neighbors that he had seen such a sight, would they not conclude that he was insane?

How can a lamb go to war?

How, then, I ask, can it be possible that a Christian, who is a partaker of Christ's Spirit and nature, and is become a harmless and defenseless lamb, can go forth to war, and, with sword and gun in hand, destroy the lives of his enemies (whom he loves); cutting them limb from limb into pieces; wasting their fields waving with beautiful grain; burning their houses and barns; destroying all the property he possibly can; making widows and orphans; and bringing sorrow and trouble, and often starvation and death upon them? Methinks the great inconsistency of a Christian, engaged in such a work as this, must be plain—yea, self-evident to every candid mind. It is certainly self-contradictory.

---

44 Philippians 2:15.
45 Genesis 18:25.

Can it be possible that a Christian, who is a partaker of Christ's Spirit and nature, and is become a harmless and defenseless lamb, can go forth to war?

Paul declares that we "do not war after the flesh; for the weapons of our warfare are not carnal." 2 Cor. 10:3, 4. The meaning of this passage must be simply this:—We Christians, who follow Christ's example, do not engage in a carnal warfare with carnal weapons: this would be ill-becoming Christ's peaceful followers, who are spiritual soldiers "using the sword of the Spirit, which is the word of God," and are fighting against their spiritual enemies, to maintain and support a spiritual, heavenly kingdom; and as no man can serve two masters, so Christians cannot be engaged in fighting for a worldly kingdom and also for a heavenly one. And oh! what a trifle is this worldly kingdom in comparison with the heavenly and everlasting kingdom! Well might the apostle say,

"The sufferings of this present time are not worthy to be compared with the glory that shall be revealed in us." Ro. 8:18. If we suffer for Christ, we shall also reign with him. If, then, Christians must suffer affliction here in this life, they know that their afflictions are but light and momentary, and work for them "a far more exceeding and eternal weight of glory; while they look not at the things which are seen, but at the things which are not seen." 2 Cor. 4:17, 18. They look with the spiritual eye, with the eye of faith, to those things which are invisible to the bodily eye: they lay up "treasures in heaven;"[46] and as Christ, the Captain of their salvation, who, though he was rich, yet for their sake became poor, so that he had not where to lay his head: even so must his followers not trust in the uncertain riches of this world—yea, they should rather suffer the spoiling of their goods, "knowing in themselves that they have in heaven a better and an enduring substance." Hebrews 10:34.

Let us look to Jesus

Therefore let Christians look to Jesus for comfort, who for the joy that was set before him, endured the cross, despising the shame. Let them consider him who, without taking revenge, endured such contradictions of sinners against himself, herein also "leaving us an example, that we should follow his steps." He was despised and rejected of men, a man of sorrows and acquainted with grief: he even suffered his enemies to spit on his holy and innocent face; he was scourged—"the plowers plowed upon his back, and made long their furrows." Ps. 129:3. They smote him in his face with the palms of their hands: they crowned him with thorns: they mocked him as a king, putting a reed in his hand, which signified a scepter, and kneeled before him, saying, "Hail King of the Jews."[47] They took the reed and smote him upon his head—they led him forth as a lamb to the slaughter, and nailed him to the cross where he suffered the most ignominious death; although he had power, that he might have prayed to his heavenly Father who would presently have given him "more than twelve legions of angels." Matt. 26:53. Yet, in all his painful agony and

---

46 Matthew 6:20.
47 Matthew 27:29; Mark 15:18; John 19:3.

suffering, he threatened not, but even prayed, saying, "Father, forgive them, for they know not what they do;"[48] thus, "leaving us an example, that we should follow his steps."

All who would live godly in Christ Jesus, must suffer persecution; as Paul says, "Being reviled we bless; being persecuted, we suffer it; being defamed, we entreat: we are made as the filth of the world, and are the offscouring of all things." 1 Cor. 4:12, 13. Such were the sufferings of the Christians in the days of the apostles, and in this they imitated their Master. Paul says, "Be ye followers of me as I am of Christ."[49] The terms of Christianity, since then, have not been changed—these same words still hold true: "If any man will come after me, let him deny himself, and take up his cross, and follow me." Never once, in the whole New Testament, do we find that the followers of Christ took up arms to slay their enemies, but many thousands of Christians since the days of the apostles have suffered martyrdom from their cruel persecutors, and for no other reason than simply because they differed from them in their religious sentiments: one point of difference among others being this, viz: that they denied that it was lawful for a Christian, according to the doctrine of Christ and his apostles, to take up arms and destroy the lives of his enemies.[50]

Christians killing Christians?

But what shall we think of those who profess to be Christians, and who belong to the same denominations and churches, some of whom are living in the North and some in the South, who are now engaged in seeking to destroy each other with the instruments of death, by thousands, on the battlefield? Are these the Christian brethren described in the New Testament? Can it be possible that these are the Christians who are born again of the Holy Spirit of Love and Peace? Or is it possible that these Christian professors are imitating Christ, by walking in his steps? Or, is Christ divided against himself? Can the love of such professors "be without

---

48   Luke 23:34.
49   1 Corinthians 11:1.
50   For proof of these facts the reader is referred to a work called "The Bloody Theater, or Martyr's Mirror."

How dreadful it is to think that men—rational creatures, made after the similitude of God—should ever tear and devour one another with a fierceness exceeding even the wild ferocious beasts of the forest!

dissimulation"[51]? Or, are they "kindly affectioned one to another?" Rom. 12:10. Can they love one another with a "pure heart, fervently," as those "being born again, not of corruptible seed, but of incorruptible, by the word of God, which liveth and abideth forever?" 1 Pet. 1:22, 23.

Now, for a moment, let us behold the scenes of a battle field, where thousands lie rolling in blood, both men and beasts, mingled together. Some dead—some just expiring—some have their arms, others their legs severed from their bodies—limbs are scattered all around, none can tell whose they were—some groaning in painful agony are wishing for death to put an end to their sufferings. Oh, what anguish, sorrow and distress! Oh, what wailing and crying for relief! Besides cannon roaring, shells bursting, muskets cracking, and the loud shout for the victory! Behold, the atmosphere is darkened with dust and smoke! Surely, here is confusion and every evil work; nor is this all, for who can describe the sorrow and distress of those at home, on receiving the sad news of the death of a dear husband—of a beloved father—a dear son or a brother? Oh, who can hear the cries of the widow and orphans weeping for their loved ones, and refusing to be comforted, because they are not!—But who can describe the dreadful evils, the painful and

---
51 Romans 12:9.

dreadful scenes and horrors of war? Can such painful and dreadful scenes be the work of Christians, those harmless, new-born lambs of Jesus? Can any of those who take a share in it be the faithful followers of him, walking in his steps? Judge ye.

I am aware that under the old Mosaical dispensation, God commanded the Jews to destroy the heathens with the sword because of their wickedness; but Christ, the Prince of peace, whom we are now to hear in all things whatsoever he bids us, gave us a new commandment, that we should love our enemies, and pray for them; which no man in the world can do, with a sincere heart, while engaged in seeking to destroy their lives—no, never, never.

There are many Mennonite brethren living both in the North and in the South. If these should, therefore, march into the field against each other, armed with swords, guns, and the most fearful instruments of death, murderously destroying one another's lives, who could believe that they were new-born persons and brethren in Christ, or that they are led by the Spirit of God? No reasonable person could believe this.[52]

How dreadful it is to think that men—rational creatures, made after the similitude of God—should ever tear and devour one another with a fierceness exceeding even the wild ferocious beasts of the forest! I think it would not be out of place here, to ask the question once asked by a woman belonging to the Society of Friends, who, it is said, arose in meeting and uttered the following impressive sentence; "I wonder what good it does men to kill their enemies? If left alone, they would die themselves."[53]

Lazarus or the rich man?

Ah, but, says one, if we would let them alone, they would come and take away from us our land and our property which we have labored so hard to gain. But I would answer in the language of the Savior, "A man's life consisteth not in the abundance of the things which he possesseth." Lu. 12:15. Again, "What would it

---
52 This paragraph is not contained in the 1863 edition; it was added in the 1868.
53 "New Contributor," "Sermon of the Quakeress," *The Knickerbocker* 30(5) (1847):437-440, p. 437.

profit a man, if he should gain the whole world and lose his own soul?" Matt. 16:26. It is true that our enemies might take away our property and destroy our bodies; but they could not destroy our souls: therefore, we are not to fear them, but to fear "Him who has power to destroy both body and soul in hell; yea, I say unto you, Fear Him."[54] Would it not, then, be the part of wisdom in us, to choose rather to have our portion in this life with Lazarus, the poor beggar, and, after death, be carried by the angels into Abraham's bosom, than to fare sumptuously with the rich man every day, and after death lift up our eyes in hell, being in torment where their worm dieth not, and their fire is not quenched?

And who would not rather, after death, receive the reward of the righteous, which is so great, than enjoy the pleasures of sin for a season? And who would not finally wish to be numbered with the great multitude which John beheld, in his Revelation, standing "before the Throne, and before the Lamb, clothed with white robes, and palms in their hands; who hunger no more, neither thirst any more?" Rev. 7:9, 16.

But he that wishes to be numbered with them, must, like them, come thither through great tribulation. The apostle says that we must, "through much tribulation, enter into the kingdom of heaven." Acts 14:22. What, if our enemies should come and take away our property? If we have the Lord on our side, we are safe: without his will not a "hair shall fall from our heads."[55] The psalmist says, "Trust in the Lord, and do good, so shalt thou dwell in the land, and verily thou shalt be fed." Ps. 37:3. He never saw the "righteous forsaken, nor his seed begging bread,"[56] "and having food and raiment, let us therewith be content." 1 Tim. 6:8. We brought nothing into this world, therefore it is very evident that we shall carry nothing out of it; and if one soul is of greater value than the whole world, what then can be gained by war? Is not the victorious party almost always the loser in the end, beyond all calculation? It is believed that even in the present (1863) struggle in our own land, less than one-half the amount that has already been

---

54 Combination of Matthew 10:28 and Luke 12:5.
55 Perhaps from Luke 21:18.
56 Psalm 37:25.

The rod of affliction has passed through the land, and many times ten thousand have been carried away as with a flood.

spent, would have preserved the peace of our country; and thus saved thousands of lives, and millions of money.

Is the war a punishment?

But who can tell, if perhaps, the sins of the American people were not so great, and the cup of their iniquity so brimful and overflowing, that the Almighty God, in his divine justice, saw proper to give "them over to a reprobate mind, to do those things which are not convenient" (Rom. 1:28)? or, perhaps, it was the object of the Almighty, that the North and the South should punish and chastise each other for their great wickedness, and withal, in the end, to do away with slavery; I say, who can tell, whether this was not the cause and the object?

God said to the Jews of old, "If ye be willing and obedient, ye shall eat of the good of the land; but if ye refuse and rebel, ye shall be devoured with the sword; for the mouth of the Lord hath spoken it." Is. 1:17, 20. But it might also be said of the people of America, as it was to the Jews, "Wherefore should ye be stricken any more? Ye will revolt more and more." Is. 1:5. Even now after the rod of affliction has passed through the land, and many times ten thousand have been carried away as with a flood, behold, what wickedness still remains in the land. Behold the excessive pride and haughtiness, the blasphemies and outrages that are daily committed! Unless America as a nation reforms, we need not be surprised at all, if the Lord will suffer his righteous judgments to be still increased upon us, for our sins, even to seven times more. Surely, judgment has not come upon us before it was fully deserved.

War not the work of Christians

Oh! what an awful scourge is war! What could be more dreadful upon the earth? It cannot be the work of Christians: they will not *make* war, and why should they engage in it afterwards? A certain writer observes, "The very spirit of war is that of hatred, and malice, and every evil passion: it is the very antagonism of the peaceful and loving spirit of the Gospel of the blessed God."[57] Another observes, "Men of conscientious scruples in religious matters have no business in the army. All conscience, all sense of right, must be laid aside by the soldier, when engaged in the art of war. Murder, rapine, theft, falsehood, cruelty, and hate, are military virtues, and the commander rewards with laurels what God forbids on pain of eternal death."[58] "War," says the same writer, "is not only a repeal of all the virtues, but also of all the sanctions of our holy religion."[59]

Now, then, since peace is one of the characteristics set forth in the prophecy of the latter day glory, when Christ, the Prince of peace, shall extend his kingdom over all the earth, let us as Christians follow after peace with all men, and holiness, without which

---

57 D. B. Cheney, "A Plea for Peace," *Advocate of Peace* 12(1) (January 1856):3-8, p. 6.
58 Excerpted from *ibid.*, p. 6. The first sentence was attributed by the article's author to the Duke of Wellington.
59 *Ibid.*, p. 7.

Christianity and War 31

no man shall see the Lord. Let the worldly-minded laugh, and scorn, and mock, as much as they please, truth will nevertheless prevail, and stand forever; although there may be produced some seemingly plausible arguments in favor of the righteousness and the justice of war, yet I feel fully persuaded in my own mind that they may be all fairly met, and refuted by the all prevailing doctrine of the Prince of peace.

I will, however, say, that if any man can prove from the doctrines and example of Jesus Christ and his apostles to a full and perfect demonstration, the justice and lawfulness of Christians going to war, and killing their enemies, then, and not till then, will I confess that I am in error, "not knowing the Scriptures."[60]

This non-resistant doctrine may seem new and strange to many, although it has been maintained and advocated for more than eighteen hundred years, by many faithful Christians; and I firmly believe, that it is the pure doctrine of Christ, which none may violate with impunity. And now, whether a Christian may take up arms, and go forth to war, and destroy the lives of his enemies, and at the same time obey the Gospel of Jesus Christ, and be justifiable in the sight of God, the Christian reader, it is hoped, will be able to decide for himself. May he "prove all things, and hold fast to that which is good."[61]

But, says one, if the doctrine of a non-resisting Christianity be a true doctrine, then there can be but few Christians in the world. Well, this is just what the Savior tells us: "Strait is the gate, and narrow is the way, which leadeth unto life; and few there be that find it."[62] "Not everyone that saith unto me, Lord, Lord, shall enter into the kingdom of heaven; but he that doeth the will of my Father, which is in heaven." Matt. 7:21. "Strive to enter in at the strait gate; for many, I say unto you, will seek to enter in, and shall not be able, when once the master of the house is risen and hath shut to the door." Lu. 13:24, 25.

---

60 Matthew 22:29.
61 1 Thessalonians 5:21.
62 Matthew 7:14.

Conclusion

In conclusion I would say to the Christian reader, should it ever be your lot to suffer persecution for conscience toward God, or for the name of Christ, or for refusing to take up arms to slay your enemies, if conscience forbids you; then think it not strange concerning such fiery trials, which are but to try you as gold is tried with fire; but look to Jesus, the Author and Finisher of your faith. He is able to protect you, and if he will not preserve your body, as he did the bodies of the three Hebrews in the burning, fiery furnace, yet will he, if you put your trust in him, preserve your soul unharmed. Christian reader! put your trust in the Lord, in all your sufferings. Be not dismayed; "for even hereunto were ye called, because Christ also suffered for us, leaving us an example that we should follow his steps."

Fellow Christian! let us be strong in the Lord and in the power of his might. Yea, let us be faithful unto death, and a crown of life will be given us. "And the ransomed of the Lord shall return and come to Zion, with songs and everlasting joy upon their heads: they shall obtain joy and gladness, and sorrow and sighing shall flee away." Is. 35:10.

Christianity and War

Christ Jesus is a Prince of peace.
His subjects peaceful too;
With them all wars must cease,
They always peace pursue.

Although despised and mocked they be
Of wicked sinners here;
They from all strife and bloodshed flee,
And walk in Jesus' fear.

As Christ their King example gave,
They rather suffer wrong;
His steps they follow to the grave,
His Spirit makes them strong.

As Christ his enemies to save,
Came down from heaven above;
So, to his own, commandment gave,
Their enemies to love.

As Christ, the true and living vine,
Is love in all his mind;
So his true branches too will shine
With fruit the same in kind.

As Christ to all example gave,
Let us, as he directs,
Fear neither storm, nor wind, nor wave,
But follow his own steps.

An Address to the Mennonite Brethren

DEAR BRETHREN:
Whereas we have now met with perilous times—times of sorrow and distress, while the whole world, as it seems, is lying in wickedness and in rebellion against God and His laws; it is surely high time for us to "awake out of sleep,"[63] and be on our guard: for we are surrounded with snares and temptations on every side, wherewith Satan is aiming to ensnare us. Let us, therefore, "watch and pray, that we fall not into temptation."[64]

And, whereas thousands are now engaged in fighting for a worldly kingdom, which is but transitory and vain; ought we not then also, who profess to seek a heavenly country, to "fight the good fight of faith,"[65] and be more vigorously engaged in fortifying ourselves against the assaults of our spiritual enemies, lest they break in upon us unawares, and rob us of our rights and privileges. Let us be as Paul writes to the Ephesians: "Finally, my brethren, be strong in the Lord, and in the power of his might. Put on the whole armor of God, that ye may be able to stand against the wiles of the devil: for we wrestle not against flesh and blood, but against principalities, against powers, against the rulers of the darkness of this world, against spiritual wickedness in high places. Wherefore, take unto you the whole armor of God, that ye may be able to withstand in the evil day, and having done all to stand. Stand, therefore, having your loins girt about with truth, and having on the breastplate of righteousness; and your feet shod with the preparation of the gospel of peace; above all, taking the shield of faith, wherewith ye shall be able to quench all the fiery darts of the wicked; and take the helmet of salvation, and the sword of the Spirit, which is the word of God: pray always with all prayer and supplication in the Spirit, and watching thereunto with all perseverance and supplication for all saints." Eph. 6:10-18. Thus we can see, my dear brethren, that a soldier of Jesus Christ must be

---

63 Romans 13:11.
64 Probably from Matthew 26:41, Mark 14:38.
65 1 Timothy 6:12.

well armed from head to foot, in order to be able to withstand the attacks of the enemy. Oh! let us not delay to seek fresh recruits, and to have them all well armed; for we may yet have hard battles to fight. Do not be discouraged, for our Captain is strong and well experienced; only follow in his footsteps—do as he bids you— keep close to his banner, and by his all powerful aid, we shall finally be more than conquerors; yea, triumphant over sin and Satan, Death and Hell.

Although we wrestle not against flesh and blood, and war not after the flesh, as the weapons of our warfare "are not carnal;"[66] yet it becomes us, nevertheless, to be *true, loyal, and faithful citizens to our worldly government in all points that do not militate against the laws of our blessed Redeemer;* and as our government has thus far allowed us freedom, and liberty of conscience, to worship God agreeably to the promptings of our most holy faith, we ought, therefore, to regard and respect our government, and earnestly and sincerely pray for its continuance; yea, we ought to support such a government in all things it may demand of us, if it be not against the pure doctrine of Christ. But should our government ask of us anything that is contrary to the Gospel of Jesus, then we must obey God rather than man. But we ought to be truly thankful to God and our government, that such provisions have thus far been made for the "Defenseless Christians," that instead of taking up arms to slay their enemies, they have always been permitted to pay an equivalent in money; and in reason we could ask no more. Oh, let us, then, all be true, loyal and faithful subjects: and whereas we cannot, for conscience sake, help uphold the government with carnal weapons, let us, at least, give to it this advantage—the assurance that it never need fear a rebellion from us;[67] and let none be in anywise injurious to the government of our

---

66 2 Corinthians 10:4.
67 The ancient Dutch Ambassador Van Benning writes to Monsieur de Turenne, "The Mennonites are a good people, and the most commodious to a state of any in the world: partly because they do not aspire to places of dignity; partly because they edify the community by the simplicity of their manners, and application to arts and industry, and partly because we fear no rebellion from a sect that makes it an article of their faith, never to bear arms."—Morgan Edwards' Life and Times of Menno, page 49.

land; but pay willingly and without murmuring all its demands and just dues, without defrauding (if we even could) in the least; knowing that, even if we could escape the punishment of men, we could not escape the punishment of God. What a self-contradiction it would be, if, after professing a nonresistant Christianity, we should be found guilty of resisting the government by rebellion and disloyalty! I would say to my ministering brethren, Expel from the church every brother that dares rebel or in any way act injuriously to the government. And, my brethren, let us not forget to pray for the government and for all those in authority, that under them, by the grace of God, "we may lead a quiet and peaceable life, in all godliness and honesty" (1 Tim. 2:2): yea, let us pray for the restoration of *peace* and *union* in our distressed and troubled country, remembering that the "effectual, fervent prayer of a righteous man availeth much." Jas. 5:16. Let us cast all our cares upon God, knowing that he careth for us, and you, my dear brethren, who are placed as watchmen over the flock, "blow the trumpet, give the alarm, be instant in season and out of season,"[68] as those who must give an account of the precious souls placed under their care; for these are alarming times.

And, oh, my dear brethren, could I only persuade you all to lay aside and banish from your minds that hurtful and baneful party spirit. Behold, what havoc it has made in our states! and now it has also entered into the churches and is separating them. Is it not enough for us to be Christians? Or must we also be called, or call ourselves, after a worldly name—a Democrat or a Republican? Surely, we ought also to guard against this evil. If we are Christians it is enough to qualify us for every duty. Oh, let no party names tear asunder the bond of love and brotherhood! We ought, by no means, to allow ourselves to be called by party names; and, oh, how shameful for Christian professors to dispute and quarrel about political matters! For those who profess to be followers of Christ, walking in his steps, and who are to be of one mind, one heart, and one soul—for one of them to say, "I am a Democrat," and another, "I am a Republican," and then to commence to dispute and quarrel with each other! I say, it is a shame for a Christian

---
68   Ezekiel 33:3; 2 Timothy 4:2.

An Address to the Mennonite Brethren

professor to do this; and I believe that a true Christian will not be guilty of such follies. And as political matters are now carried on to extremes—to excess—beyond the bounds of reason and religion, I would say, Stand aloof! Keep at a proper distance and within the bounds of Christianity! Dear brethren, suffer yourselves to be persuaded and convinced of the inconsistency of nonresistant professors taking part in worldly elections, and in the choosing of worldly rulers. Is it not overstepping the bounds of a non-resistant Christianity, when we help choose men into office in which it becomes their duty to use deadly weapons? Is it not, then, plain that whosoever does this, acts in opposition to the non-resistant principles and their profession? Therefore,[69] be separate and touch not the unclean thing—run not with others "to the same excess of riot" (1 Pet. 4:4); and let our moderation in this respect "be known unto all men." Phil. 4:5.

Let us, by our walk and conversation, declare plainly, that we seek a heavenly country; and let us not be entangled with the trifles and follies of this present evil world, as to neglect the "one thing needful."[70] Surely, a man may be useful in upholding and supporting the government, without going beyond the bounds of reason and sense. Let us seek more those things which are above, having our "conversation (or walk) in heaven,"[71] and letting our "light shine before men, that they may see our good works."[72] Let us be good and kind to all who stand in need, especially at this time. Let us not forget the widows and the orphans, but open to them our hearts and hands, and not only say to them, "Be ye warmed and filled," but give them what is "needful for the body." Jas. 2:16. Oh, let us live as Christians: in love, peace, and union. Let us build up each other in our "most holy faith,"[73] and let us "follow after the things which make for peace and things wherewith one may edify another." Phil. 4:19. "Finally, brethren, be per-

---

69 These sentences, beginning with "Dear brethren, suffer yourselves..." are not in the 1863 edition, but were added in the 1868.
70 Luke 10:42.
71 Philippians 3:20.
72 Matthew 5:16.
73 Jude 1:20.

fect, be of good comfort, be of one mind, live in peace, and the God of love and peace shall be with you." 2 Cor. 13:11.

I will go in the strength of the Lord. Ps. 71:16.

Trust in the Lord forever; for in the Lord Jehovah is everlasting strength. Is. 26:4.[74]

> Be strong, my brethren dear,
> Be strong, and never fear
> The rage of war.
> Oh! fight and watch and pray,
> Your *inward* foes to slay,
> Who meet you in the way,
> Your hopes to mar.
>
> Be strong in Christ the Lord,
> Who kindly in his word
> Says, Do not fear.
> Fear not, he says to you,
> Those who your life pursue;
> 'Tis all that they can do,
> If God be near.
>
> Be strong in Christ your Tower,
> And in his mighty power,
> Ye Christians all.
> His mighty arm can save
> You from the storm and wave,
> And from an early grave,
> Both great and small.
>
> Be strong! O yes, be strong!
> Your suff'rings can't be long,
> Ye little band.
> The night is almost gone,
> The day will shortly come,
> When saints shall reach their home
> At Christ's right hand.

---

[74] These final two Scriptures are not in the 1863 edition, but were added in the 1868.

An Address to the Mennonite Brethren

Be strong in faith and love—
Let all your actions prove
Your hearts sincere:
Be kind and good to those
Who your good will oppose—
Yes, pray for all your foes:
Your God will hear.

Be strong, and murmur not
Though suff'ring be your lot;
'Tis thus the Lord
Designs to make us clean,
Our sinful hearts to wean
From all that tempts to sin—
Oh trust his word.

Be strong, though faint you be,
And sorrow presseth thee
On every side.
Sufficient is God's grace,
Your fainting hopes to raise,
That you can sing his praise,
Whate'er betide.

Be strong, and never fear,
Though, every day, you hear
News stain'd with blood.
For needs these things must be,
As in God's word we see—
"Do not affrighted be,"
Says Christ, your Lord.

A Word to the Careless

"What meanest thou, O sleeper? arise, call upon thy God."
Jonah 1:6.

These[75] alarming words were addressed to the prophet Jonah, to whom came the word of the Lord saying: "Arise, go to Nineveh; that great city, and cry against it; for their wickedness is come up before me. But Jonah rose up to flee unto Tarshish from the presence of the Lord, and went down to Joppa; and he found there a ship going to Tarshish: so he paid the fare thereof and went down into it, to go with them unto Tarshish from the presence of the Lord. But the Lord sent out a great wind into the sea, and there was a mighty tempest in the sea, so that the ship was like to be broken. Then the mariners were afraid, and cried every man unto his God:" "But Jonah was gone down into the sides of the ship; and he lay, and was fast asleep. So the shipmaster came to him and said unto him, What meanest thou, O sleeper? arise, call upon thy God, if so be that God will think upon us, that we perish not."[76]

The case of Jonah is a true representation of a careless and thoughtless sinner. He went down into the sides of the ship, and lay there, fast asleep, while the wind was blowing fiercely, and the tempest wildly raging; and the billows were rolling, and heaving and rocking the frail, little ship, now to this side, now to that side; and threatening every moment to dash her to pieces amid the fearful storm, and leave her, and all on board to perish forever beneath the raging waters; little thinking, and knowing nothing of the danger he was in. The mariners had already become conscious of their danger, and cast forth the wares of the ship, to lighten her, and made every preparation to enable her to withstand the great tempest, but finding all their efforts to help themselves in vain, they yielded in despair of their own strength, and "cried every man to

---

75 This essay is only in the 1863 edition.
76 Jonah 1:6.

his God,"⁷⁷ and all this time, unconscious, and unconcerned as a child, Jonah, the prophet of the Lord, lay sleeping in the sides of the ship, a fugitive, seeking to flee from the presence of his God, while at every moment he was in danger of sinking to the bottom of the sea, even in his sleep—lost! lost! lost, in his sleep of the body—lost, in his sleep of the soul—lost, in his disobedience and his disregard of the word of the Lord which came to him, commanding him to go and bear the message of the wrath of the Lord to the wicked and disobedient Ninevites.

Just so it is with the sinner before he is brought to a knowledge of sin. He, like Jonah, is a wanderer, a fugitive from his God: though the word of the Lord may have come unto him, time after time; again and again he may have been called upon to repent—to return from his wanderings in sin—to awake out of his sleep and call upon his God, yet disregarding all, he is apt to say with the sluggard: "Yet a little sleep, a little slumber, a little folding of the hands to sleep,"⁷⁸ not knowing, not thinking that as Jonah, "fast asleep" in the side of the little ship upon the Mediterranean Sea was in danger of sinking to the bottom, and perishing forever under its surging waves, so he is in great danger of sinking into the bottomless pit—into the "lake burning with fire and brimstone"⁷⁹, and perishing there, both body and soul in hell, forever—"where the worm dieth not and the fire is not quenched,"⁸⁰ "which is the second death."⁸¹

All such careless, and unawakened sinners, I would address in the language of the ship-master, "What meanest thou, O sleeper?" O! what canst thou mean! thou hast an immortal soul to save or to lose forever. O! what meanest thou? "awake thou that sleepest and arise from the dead."⁸² Arise to newness of life, for thus must the sinner rise from the death of sin—from the death of his natural life, to a new, spiritual, a heavenly life—thus through a spiritual

---

77   Jonah 1:5.
78   Proverbs 6:10; 24:33.
79   Revelation 19:20.
80   Mark 9:44, 46, 48.
81   Revelation 21:8.
82   Ephesians 5:14.

resurrection must he rise and "pass from death unto life,"[83] even in this world: And, "if ye then be risen with Christ, seek those things which are above."[84]

Arise therefore, and call upon thy God, "for whosoever shall call upon the name of the Lord shall be saved."[85]—The Lord is nigh unto all that call upon him, unto all that call upon him in truth. "Why sleep ye? rise and pray,"[86] was the language of the Saviour to his disciples in the garden of Gethsemane. "Seek ye the Lord while he may be found, call upon him while he is near."[87] How often, O Sinner, is he near unto thee, knocking at the door of your heart! Rise therefore, "he calleth thee."[88] He called thee that thou shouldst turn from thy ways of sin, come back from thy wanderings, return from the path of evil and disobedience, and "call upon thy God, if so be that God will think upon thee and thou perish not."[89] He is able and willing, O sinner, to save thee from thy lost and perishing condition. He is "not willing that any should perish, but that all should come to repentance."[90] O sinner, what meanest thou! it is now "high time to awake out of sleep,"[91] thy end is nigh, there is but a step between thee and death. Awake then, O sinner; "Repent and be converted, that your sins may be blotted out, when the time of refreshing shall come."[92]—"Except ye be converted and become as little children," said the Saviour, "ye shall not enter into the kingdom of heaven;"[93] and again: "Except a man be born again he cannot see the kingdom of God."[94] Dear sinner, would you not wish to see the kingdom of God, and enter therein, to be eternally happy, with saints and angels there? O! prepare then to meet thy God, for none but God's children can

---

83   John 5:24; 1 John 3:14.
84   Colossians 3:1.
85   Acts 2:21.
86   Luke 22:46.
87   Isaiah 55:6.
88   Mark 10:49.
89   Jonah 1:6.
90   2 Peter 3:9.
91   Romans 13:11.
92   Acts 3:19.
93   Matthew 18.3.
94   John 3:3.

A Word to the Careless 43

ever enter into His kingdom. "What meanest thou then, O sleeper, arise, call upon thy God,"—call upon Him to "create a clean heart, and renew a right spirit within you."[95] Call upon him for mercy—call upon him in the name of Jesus for the forgiveness of your sins—call upon Him that thou perish not; yea: "Let the wicked forsake his way, and the unrighteous man his thoughts, and let him return unto the Lord, and he will have mercy upon him, and to our God, for he will abundantly pardon."[96]

Verily, verily, I say unto thee
"Except a man be born again"
God's kingdom he can never see,
Nor e'er to happiness attain.

This is the doctrine of the Lord,
Which he to Nicodemus gave—
The apostles too, with one accord
To this reviving doctrine clave.

"How can man old, be born again,"
Said Nicodemus;—"tell me this."
But Jesus Christ now told him plain:
"Of water and the Spirit 'tis."

The Spirit is from God above,—
The fount of living water pure,
Who is a God of truth and love;
And whose promises are all sure.

---

95 Psalm 51:10.
96 Isaiah 55:7.

Appendix

Warfare: Its Evils, Our Duty

Addressed to the
Mennonite Churches
throughout the
United States and Canada,
and all others who
sincerely seek and
love the truth

By John F. Funk

Preface

It is well known that the members of our Church have always been a non-resistant people; indeed, this principle has ever been a feature, so prominently brought out and sustained, that before the days of Menno[97] and Waldo[98] our sect was known as the "DEFENCELESS CHRISTIANS."[99] We sincerely and conscientiously believe, that according to the Gospel, as taught and practiced by Jesus Christ, no man can so far infringe the laws of heaven and nature, and the instincts of a common humanity, as to engage in legalized murder and robbery, and still retain the love of God in his heart.

We cannot pray for the destruction of our fellow men, even though they be our enemies, for Christ says, "Love your enemies;"[100] but we MAY pray—it is our privilege, yea, our duty to pray—that God will let the light of his blessed Gospel shine upon them, and give them light, that they may see the error of their ways, and turn back to the allegiance of both their God and their Government. But we all have great need to pray for ourselves, that we may not fall in the same error of which we accuse others.

In these times of war and blood-shed, we, as members of a Christian Church, sustaining these principles of a Universal Peace, are placed in peculiarly trying circumstances. Some may have forgotten their duty and grown cold and indifferent—others may be discouraged, and some may have laid aside these sacred principles altogether, to follow that which is wrong and unrighteous before God; if such is the case with any, who may read the words which I have written, think they have been written for you, and if they awaken in your heart a warmer devotion to your God and your religion; if they bring your duties anew to your mind and speak words of hope and encouragement to your soul; if they, perchance,

---

97   Menno Simons (c. 1496-1561), a Dutch Anabaptist church leader after whom the Mennonite church was named.—*Ed.*
98   Waldesius, better known as Peter Waldo, after whom the Waldensians were named.—*Ed.*
99   Funk apparently accepted the idea that the Anabaptists came from the Waldensians, and that the Waldensians could be traced back to the time of the apostles.—*Ed.*
100   Matthew 5:44; Luke 6:27; see also Luke 6:35.—*Ed.*

should lead you back from error's ways to paths of rectitude and holiness, or in any manner bring you nearer to God, and make you stronger in faith, and hope, and truth, I shall feel that these words have not been written in vain. May God's blessing go with them!

Warfare:
Its Evils—Our Duty

Then said Jesus unto him, Put up again thy sword into his place, for all they that take the sword, shall perish with the sword.
Math. xxvi. 52.

War, in all ages of the world, has been the almost universal scourge of mankind. The destruction of human life and property from this one fearful and gigantic source of evil alone, is, at this day, beyond the power of human calculation to estimate. In every age of the world, in every land, and under every government, Satan, the father of wars, as he is the father of lies, has led forth his cohorts to the work of blood and death, devastation and destruction; and in their train followed. O! who can conceive or form the remotest idea of the misery, the woe, the bitter anguish, the wail of sorrow, and the cry of despair, the distress and poverty and pain, that have evinced themselves in every war since time began. The crimson life current has flowed in streams dark and deep over all the earth; and to-day, with the sad memories of a thousand battlefields, that come up before our minds, as we follow the records of history, in the ages past, we realize that the avenger is abroad in our own midst, and the sword, dyed deep in the blood of our own brethren, kinsmen, and countrymen, is yet raised against our own selves, threatening destruction of our lives, the desolation of our homes, and the ruin of our country, our government—the land we love, and cherish, and hold dear.

Amid such scenes and circumstances, it is very natural for us to follow the ways of the world, and add constant fuel to the already fast devouring flames. Our hearts are inclined to sin, to resentment, to unrighteousness; and we, instead of bringing ourselves under subjection to the law of Christ; give loose reins to our passions, and follow our sinful desires and inclinations; and instead of separating ourselves and standing aloof from all the vain honors of the world, as Christ became our example, we feel that we must have a part in all these worldly gratifications and pleasures; we wish to share in them; but those who share in the labors, and the pleasures, and the triumphs of sinful men, must also share in their reward.

Thus, for instance, rises a great military hero. He comes to us with garments red with human gore. He has made himself the greatest murderer of the age, the most extensive robber in all the land. At his command hundreds and thousands of precious lives have been laid cold in death; in his victorious train follows the widows' wail, the orphans' cry, blasted hopes and blighted pros-

> The humble follower of the meek and lowly Jesus, in unassuming garb, in all lowliness of heart, and meekness of spirit, goes about doing good to all.

pects; and when he is gone, there remain the ashes and the dust of burned and ruined cities, desolated homes, devastated fields, and mourning hearts throughout the land, weeping in bitter agony for the loved ones lost in the bloody strife; but we say a great man, a mighty conqueror—he has performed great and noble deeds, he has accomplished mighty ends; he deserves our honor, our praise, our homage; and freely we bestow it, and bow before him with a warmer devotion than we bow before the throne of the Ruler of the Universe. And all this we do, forgetting altogether the humble follower of the meek and lowly Jesus, who, in unassuming garb, unostentatiously, in all lowliness of heart, and meekness of spirit, goes about doing good to all, seeking to keep God's commandments and do his will; endeavoring to cultivate the arts of peace in his own heart, and promulgate them among others; following close in the footsteps of his Master, and never aspiring to anything other than the honor of God, the happiness of his fellow man, and

Warfare: Its Evils—Our Duty

the salvation of his own soul; he is forgotten and neglected by us all, passed by unobserved and unnoticed, and by many of us despised, mocked, and even persecuted—laughed to scorn; left lying like Lazarus at the rich man's gate, without one sympathizing word from human lips to cheer him on his way, denied even the crumbs that fall from the master's table; and yet how much more does he deserve our honor, our affection, our support, and our encouragement? And how much more worthy is he of our regard than the man who, through seas of blood, and over the slain bodies of our own countrymen, has lifted himself to receive the homage of the world? Jesus says he that is least among you all, the same shall be great,[101] and if you love me, keep my commandments[102]: by this shall all men know that ye are my disciples, if ye love one another.[103] The wise man, Solomon, declares, that he that ruleth his own spirit, is better than he that taketh a city.[104] David could not built the temple because he was a man of war, and had shed blood; but Solomon was a man of peace, and builded a house unto the Lord. Oh! false hearted and deluded people that we are; we worship the works of the evil one, and despise the works of God; we honor and glorify wicked and sinful men, and justify their evil works, while we forget God, and look with scorn and contempt upon him who gave his life for us, and who, in his dying hour, prayed for his murderers, saying, "Father, forgive them, for they know not what they do."[105]

Christian reader! I ask you, when will you learn to justify, and encourage, and follow the blessed religion of the meek and lowly Jesus, which he came down from heaven to establish? When will you cease to let your heart go out after the things of this world, and devote all your strength to the things of God, and the salvation of your soul?

We all have some kind of religion, but it is a sad thought that the religion of many, yea, of most men, is not the religion of Jesus, but of the devil. It is a dark and dismal worship of the natural

---

101 Luke 9:48.
102 John 14:15.
103 John 13:35.
104 Proverbs 16:32.
105 Luke 23:34.

inclinations of our hearts, going out after this world in the vain and deceptive idea that we are worshipping God, and keeping his commandments; while the love of God, and love towards our fellow man, even towards our enemies—without which no man can serve the Lord, and by which all men shall know that we are Christ's disciples—is not in us. We are deceiving ourselves; of such Christ says, "many shall say to me Lord, Lord, and shall not enter into the kingdom of heaven."[106]

Our land, which has so long been to us a land of peace, where, under the mercy of God, and the gracious care of his own right hand, and the protection of his laws, and the laws of our land, we have sat down under our own vine and fig tree, and worshipped him according to the prompting of our own hearts, none daring to molest us, or to make us afraid, is submerged in blood.—The corruption and the wickedness of the people, and the spirit of resentment and revenge, so long cherished by them, has led on the people of the south against the people of the north; and in turn the people of the north against those of the south, until the passions of each became so fired, that both parties were ready for war; and then the war came. The sword was unsheathed, and the brave men of the land, misled by false teachers, and deluded in their judgments, went forth by the hundred thousand to fight, and bleed, and die, in the sad work of destroying one another.

Thousands have been maimed and cut, as it were, limb from limb, and thousands more lie cold in death, and still the work goes on—still the contending armies, in the mad rage of human wrath, are seeking to gain the laurels of victory, and the glory of the conqueror in the red life blood of their own brethren; and the question comes home to our own hearts, shall we also take a part in this fratricidal strife? Shall we, who are the professed followers of the Prince of Peace, lay aside reason and religion, give way to our passions, and bear the sword to execute the judgments which belong to God alone?

It is a question of grave importance, which we should well consider with deep studied thought and earnest prayer. The language of the Bible on this point, however, is clear and explicit. "Do vio-

---
106   Matthew 7:21-22; 18:3.

lence to no man."[107] "If a man smite thee on thy right cheek, turn to him the other also."[108] This is the language of our Saviour himself, whom we acknowledge as our King. He is called the Prince of Peace. The prophets of old declared, before his coming, that his reign shall be a reign of peace, and his people shall beat their swords into ploughshares, and their spears into pruning hooks; nation shall not lift up sword against nation, neither shall they learn war any more. At his birth, angel messengers came from heaven, and with a multitude of the heavenly host sang, "Glory to God in the highest, and on earth PEACE AND GOOD WILL TO MAN."[109] In his sermon on the mount he says, "Blessed are the peace-makers:

> Christ pronounces a blessing upon the peace-makers, but in no place do we find a single word of hope or encouragement for those who disturb and destroy peace, create dissension and ill feeling, or riot and war.

for they shall be called the children of God."[110] Mark, Christ pronounces a blessing upon the peace-makers, but in no place do we find a single word of hope or encouragement for those who disturb and destroy peace, create dissension and ill feeling, or riot and war. To Peter he speaks in the language of the text, "Put up again thy sword into his place, for all they that take the sword, shall perish with the sword;"[111] and when arraigned before the Jewish

---

107 Luke 3:14.
108 Matthew 5:39 paraphrase.
109 Luke 2:14 paraphrase.
110 Matthew 5:9.
111 Matthew 26:52.

governor, Pilate,[112] he said, "My kingdom is not of this world; if my kingdom were of this world, then would my servants fight, that I should not be delivered to the Jews; but now is my kingdom not from hence."[113]—When scourged, and mocked, and crowned with thorns, and spat upon, he bore it meekly, and humbly—when railed and reviled by the Jewish multitude, he looked upon them in pitying silence; and when nailed to the cross, he lifted his dying voice to heaven and with bitterest agony in his soul, cried out, "Father, forgive them, for they know not what they do."[114] And thus was his whole life a noble, a glorious, an ever living illustration of the truth and the application of his words—his own doctrines and instructions.—Always the same meek and lowly Jesus, patient, forbearing, long-suffering, kind, loving and forgiving; never angry, never resenting, never injuring, never wronging any one; not returning evil for evil, but overcoming evil with good, blessing even his enemies, and praying for his cruel murderers.

Such was the life of Jesus, and now his divine injunction to us is this: "If any man will be my disciple, let him deny himself, and take up his cross and follow me."[115] This is the imperative and unavoidable duty of every Christian man, and woman, and child, who desires an inheritance in the kingdom of the Redeemer—to follow closely in his footstep, and to endeavor day by day, to become more like him—to exercise and cultivate all those Christian graces, which through all his life he so wonderfully displayed in their fullest perfection—we must make them our constant study—reach out after them, cherish and cultivate them, that they may grow stronger, and that we may approach nearer to him, until, like the full grown, and well ripened ear of corn, we may be prepared for the great harvest of life, and then the morning of eternal beauty shall dawn, and we be transplanted to that glorious clime, where we shall reign with him forever.

---

112 Pilate was a Roman governor, not Jewish; Funk may have meant that Pilate was a governor of the Jewish people.—*Ed.*
113 John 18:36.
114 Luke 23:34.
115 Paraphrased from such verses as Matthew 16:24, Mark 8:34, & Luke 9:23.

Warfare: Its Evils—Our Duty 53

Now let us for a moment compare the spirit of the warrior, and him who bears the sword, with the life, and spirit, and doctrine of our Saviour.

The warrior takes the sword in his hand to execute judgment for himself, in his own way. "Vengeance is mine, I will repay, saith the Lord."[116] Thus breaking God's commandment at once.

Again, the spirit of a soldier is a spirit of wrath, resentment, and revenge,—eye for an eye, tooth for a tooth, evil for evil, life for life; all in direct opposition to the law and the instruction of the Gospel. One fundamental principle in the Christian life is forgiveness.—How can I forgive my enemy, and fulfill the law of Christ, when with sword in hand I go sworn to kill him?

Again, Christ says, "Love your enemies. Bless them that curse you, do good to them that hate you, and pray for them that despitefully use you and persecute you; that ye may be the children of your Father, which is in Heaven, for he maketh his Sun to rise on the evil and on the good, and sendeth rain on the just, and on the unjust."[117]

Can I love my enemy so much, as to believe it my Christian duty, to go out and meet him with the full determination of killing him, if I am able? Can I love him so much, or so little, I should say, as to be impelled to go forth, and do him all the injury I can—take his property, or destroy it,—burn his house—desolate his fields, and even destroy his life, and ask God to bless me in the work; when he has commanded me to forgive, even as I would be forgiven, and exercise charity to all men—even to turning my left cheek to him who has stricken me on the right. No, Christian Reader, there can be no Christianity in warfare,—it is a simple contradiction of terms, and the difference between the two is as wide as the distance between Heaven and Hell—the one has no dealings, no affinity, with the other. Christ says: Love your enemies, &c., that ye may be the children of God: thus implying that a child of God must of necessity love its enemies, and exercise all other Christian virtues. Then, if I love not my enemies, I can be no child of God. If I bear the sword in destruction of my enemy, I cannot love him,

---

116 Romans 12:19.
117 Matthew 5:44-45.

and hence can be no child of God, and have no salvation, and no heirship with Christ, who died to save me.

Christ is our example. He never took the sword, he never taught his disciples to fight; but, to his followers he said, if they persecute you in one city, flee ye into another[118]; and the followers of these blessed Bible principles, through the dark ages of the world, suffered persecution and death in the most cruel ways, for their faithfulness to their religion; and Menno, the illustrious reformer and founder of our own sect, held fast to the true doctrines, and faithfully taught them wherever he went; and it is our duty to sustain them, and abide by them. Let us not forget nor neglect them; they are the true principles of the true religion of Jesus—without them we cannot please God, and our worship is only a mockery—sacrilege,—but this imposes upon us a trying duty, a duty which God alone can help us to perform; there are many embarrassments in our way—we must meet the scoffs, the jeers, and abuses of the world, but Christ bore the same—and we are not better than he. Let us do our duty wherever and whatever that duty be; if danger, and hardship, and exposure be in the way, never mind, put your trust in God, he will give you strength, and lift you up out of the miry places, and set your feet upon the Rock of Ages. Oh! let us do our duty to God and man and be faithful to the end, though sorrow and suffering, trial and tribulation, and even death stand in the way—never mind, let us meet them bravely, nobly, trusting still in God for help. He is our high Rock and our strong Tower; those who put their trust in Him, shall never be dismayed nor confounded. If we are only sincere and earnest, our prayers will avail and He will help us, even through the dark valley and the deep river; under the shadow of His wing will He keep us, until we reach the farther shore, and stand where the Sun of Righteousness shall arise with healing on his wings, and the darkness of sin and death shall overshadow us no more; where wars, and rumors of wars, shall be heard never again; where all strife, and hatred, and passion, and trouble, shall forever cease, and where the weary are at rest.

---

118   Matthew 10:23.

Oh, God of mercy, let our cries,
Unto thy throne of light ascend;
Cast on the earth thy gracious eyes,
And bid this wild contention end.

Behold the world thou mad'st so fair—
Its brightest spots are stained with gore,
The smell of carnage taints the air,
The waves are red from shore to shore.

Behold beneath the blessed sun,
In Freedom's wronged and outraged name,
How hell itself is far outdone,
In shouts and shrieks, in smoke and flame.

One word of thine, oh, God of love,
This tide of blood will staunch,—
Send forth, O Lord, another dove
To bear another olive branch.

Sources for Further Study

Brenneman, John M. "A Civil War Petition to President Lincoln." *Mennonite Historical Bulletin* 34(4) (October 1973):2-3.

Brenneman, John M. "Cover Letter to Petition." *Mennonite Historical Bulletin* 34(4) (October 1973):3.

Liechty, Joseph, and James O. Lehman. "From Yankee to Nonresistant: John F. Funk's Chicago Years, 1857-1865." *Mennonite Quarterly Review* 59(3) (July 1985):203-247.

Lehman, James O., and Steven M. Nolt. *Mennonites, Amish, and the American Civil War*. 2007. Johns Hopkins University Press.

Also by John M. Brenneman

Encouragement to Penitent Sinners

Nothing can be more needful, and nothing should interest a sinner more deeply, than a true conversion to God. Upon this depends his eternal well-being! A sinner under conviction should have a correct and clear understanding of true conversion so that he be not led astray by the deception of a false conversion. This books aims to reveal true Gospel conversion in as plain and comprehensive manner as is possible, so that no convicted sinner will, after reading it, have reason to complain that the subject is too dark, mysterious, and unintelligible.

Pride and Humility

Pride.
Who hasn't faced this destructive evil ... right in his own heart? Pride is so elusive. Just when we think we have escaped its grasp, we suddenly come to realize that we may be proud of the fact that we are not proud! And like the Pharisee in Jesus' parable, we begin to think evil of publicans who are beneath our self-appraised dignity.
This book is an attempt to teach us humility, so that God's grace may flow in—and out—of us.

For more excellent titles and other material by the same author, call or write for a free catalog:

Sermon on the Mount Publishing
P.O. Box 246
Manchester, MI 48158
(734) 428-0488

the-witness@sbcglobal.net

www.kingdomreading.com

www.ingramcontent.com/pod-product-compliance
Lightning Source LLC
Chambersburg PA
CBHW071915070526
44583CB00016B/1994